POEMS OF WILLIAM T. COSTELLO, S.J.

Edited by

Helen Costello Petrich

*For Colleen Mulligan,
for your kindness
Helen C. Petrich*

Reid Printing   Tacoma, Washington

ISBN 0-9629578-3-6

Library of Congress Card Catalog Number: 67-25669

Copyright © by William T. Costello

All Rights Reserved

First Edition 1968

Second Edition 1993

Published by Reid Printing, Inc.

2552 South Jefferson, Tacoma, WA 98402

To our parents
Bartley and Catherine Costello
with love and gratitude from your children

Bill
Mary
Catherine
Frank
Helen
Joe
Therese

William T. Costello, S.J.

Father Costello was born November 29th, 1914 in Spokane, Washington. He was the eldest child of seven born to Bartley and Catherine Costello.

Father Costello entered the Society of Jesus, Oregon Province, in 1932 and was ordained in San Francisco in 1944.

After receiving his Master's Degree from Gonzaga University in Spokane, he was awarded a doctorate in English Literature from Harvard University in 1953.

He was a Fulbright Scholar at Emmanuel College, Cambridge University where his research centered on the literature of the 17th Century. His doctoral thesis "The Curriculum at Seventeenth Century Cambridge" was published by the Harvard Press.

At the time of his death in 1963, Father Costello was Chairman of the English Department at Gonzaga University.

Some comments about Father Costello and his poems after their first publication in 1968

I remember so well his gusty imagination, his love, his humanity and his deep philosophy and faith.

> Ronald G.W. Norrish
> Nobel laureate and Father
> Costello's close friend and
> professor at Emmanuel College,
> Cambridge

Some part of his vision was like Emily Dickinson's; and some of his images remind me of her awesome childlike challenges.

> Albert Van Nostrand
> Member of the English
> Department , Brown University

...this merry, this perceptive and generous heart.

> Excerpt from the homily at the
> Solemn Requiem Mass for
> Father Costello, stated by John
> P. Leary, S.J.

...wonderful in his joyousness, his love for all sorts and conditions of men, the generosity of his praise, and the modesty of his own claims to eminence. Of such truly are the kingdom of heaven.

> Howard Mumford Jones
> Abbott Lawrence Lowell
> Professor of Humanities
> Harvard University

CONTENTS

1

II : OF NATURE

2

III : OF GOD

MY BROTHER, FATHER COSTELLO

I would like to write a few words about my brother Bill, the late Father William T. Costello, S.J. Perhaps it can help you to know what kind of man he was.

He was, first of all, a devoted Jesuit priest. He had an enormous love of God, especially as evidenced in the Blessed Trinity. This love extended to his fellow men, most profoundly to the poor and the forgotten. He often asked his Jesuit superiors to send him to skid road on Christmas Eve where he ministered to the least remembered of all.

Bill was the eldest of the seven children of Bartley and Catherine Costello. He was a warmly affectionate son and brother, and his tender concern followed us even after we were grown.

He was a sensitive poet; a brilliant, meticulous scholar and teacher, yet he was down to earth.

When he was a boy he worked, variously, as a farm hand on a wheat ranch, on the railroad; and he spent one hot memorable summer working in a box factory. He never forgot what it means to have to earn a living.

Bill knew periods of depression and desolation. But most of his friends remember him as a gentle and a merry man.

To sum up my brother's life most accurately is to say simply: Bill Costello loved God.

February 21, 1966   HELEN COSTELLO PETRICH
Tacoma, Washington

FATHER WILLIAM T. COSTELLO, S.J.

It will be a long time again before a man of the sensitivity and rather rare genius of Father Bill Costello comes to Gonzaga. Though he is dead now these four years, his memory, and more than that, is as fresh and warm as if we had seen him only yesterday. He had unusual gifts, not the least of which was his deep understanding of people. Simple, ordinary, different people. And when he became empathic, as he so often did, he typified that kind of Irishman whose laughter was not too far from tears and vice versa.

I know I speak for all the Gonzaga community when I salute this remarkable man who comes alive again in this book. His poetry is like a song and all of us are glad that we have known this man as friend and brother. The world really was enriched by his living and, strangely enough, by his dying.

John P. Leary, S.J.
President
Gonzaga University

March 7, 1967
Spokane, Washington

THIRTY YEARS LATER

It has been 30 years since my brother, Father William T. Costello S.J., died on May 5, 1963.

A whole generation of poetry writers and readers have been born, and, grown to adulthood, are puzzled and searching and in need, it seems, of the quiet compassion and assurance of God's love for them found in these poems.

Meanwhile, I have reached three score and ten years. And in my growing and knowing have found my own generation looking for the same reassurances.

In fact, the whole human race appears hungry for just the sort of message my brothers' poems send: vast hope, the belief in the absolute necessity of laughter and the sure knowledge that God loves each of us tenderly and abundantly especially in those places of our hearts where we hurt most.

It is a magnificent legacy—brother Bill—thank you for leaving it to us. After 30 years your words still ring true.

I pass your message on with a full and joyous heart.

HELEN C. PETRICH
July, 1993

Foreward

On reading the Poems of Father Costello one will be instantly struck by the kinship they bear to Japanese Haiku or seventeen-syllable poems. The tiny verse form which was favored by the great poets of seventeenth and eighteenth century Japan — by Basho, Sokan, Yaha Boncho and others—has influenced Western verse in content as well as form and the term vignette comes instantly to mind when one seeks an English equivalent for the kind of brief poem that seems to hover lightly over the thought which it contains, barely touching it and then, all at once, reveals a wealth of hidden meaning, and a wholly unexpected loveliness.

All of the poems in this volume are like that—seemingly strangely fugitive, etched with the lightest of brush strokes and yet, just as surely, evocative and profound.

They are not, however, oriental in mood or theme. There is a preoccupation here with orthodox Christianity and Western philosophical thought and that, combined with the brevity just mentioned, is what makes these poems so perceptive and unusual.

They are poems of joy as well as of sorrow, and they strike chords familiar to us all—hauntingly beautiful for the most part and marked by a truly startling originality.

The volume abounds in memorable lines and thought-provoking imagery.

Pervasive in all of these poems is a religious faith so firmly centered in God's abiding love and a feeling of Oneness with the Eternal that Father Costello can permit himself brief moments of all too human uncertainty and even of doubt. Such moments have a way of strengthening belief, as all of the mystics and Saints have attested, and that surely applies to poets as well.

OF MAN

Double-take Him

Everything I try is somehow said
More deftly and more meaningfully before.
I write of birds and grass and heroes dead,
Of private woes, my lady's pinafore,

Of God, his grace, the clouded autumn sky,
Heels, hearts, hopes, hurts—so better they.
Yet none has ever better said than I
How better's everybody else's say.

Men of Tarawa

Brave men of Tarawa
From Oregon, from Arkansas,
Brave men of Tarawa
Tell us why you died.

Tell the vision that you saw,
Brave men of Tarawa,
Broken little wisps of straw
Ebbing on the tide.

For Robert Frost

Dear tousle-headed piece of oak,
Who took the little things of earth
And made them speak through you, who spoke
Of wall and woodpile, road and birth
And death.

Dear tousle-headed, lying stark,
Look you now on Abora,
And Arden Forest, Shelley's lark,
And the Tabard Inn. And draw
A breath.

Spring in Middle Age

Despite it's spring
I miss the sound of children's laughter,
Hop-scotch games and squares, and marbles
(Fist-fights after).

Am I too old?
Or is it because the skeins of middle age have
                  now just caught us?
Make us blind to them?
Years have not taught us?

To a Young Lady after Lunch

How bright you were,
A thing of dew.
Was it one
Or half-past two?

A meeting that
In afterward
Is hardly said
And scarcely heard.

I laughed tonight!
And no one else would laugh with me.
I laughed and smelled the sweetness of the earth.
And thought
How God, kings, president,
Concerned with little men,
Like me,
Are self-concerned.

Loverly

I love families all around me;
I love women who surround me;
I love men;
And then
And most and odd
I love God.

About a Saint

I met a saint.
He said to me,
"The more of Him,
The less I be."

I heard him out.
And after him
Came tumbling little
Cherubim.

Good Men Are Old Wine

Deep in tender cellars
Good wine keeps and keeps
Until in shattered fragments
It sleeps, and sleeps and sleeps.

August 3, 1492

Put her out to sea, men, work her off the roadstead!
Up the hook and off the lines to shore!
Heave her out to windward where the waves will roll her
Wind and rain and rain and wind...West more!

Steer her west by sou'west fair into the sunset
Brilliant out beyond:—the world's astern—
Send the men aloft there, give her every shred, men!
Helm to lee, my man, a quarter turn...

Crazy, daft Colombo, sailing out from Palos
Life's a flimsy thing of planks and spars.
Crazy, daft Colombo? Crazy those in safe beds!
Gone where none but God has seen the stars!

Psalm CCCLX

The dishes in my little sink include
The world I came to live in, simply viewed.

My unmade beds, my front room, phones include
The world I came to live in, simply viewed.

My mothers' club, my husband's friends include
The world I came to live in, simply viewed.

My third son's hurt and hospital include
The world I came to live in, simply viewed.

My oldest's anguishings in love include
The world I came to live in, simply viewed.

And me, poor me, can You at last include
Me, mine, him, theirs (Yours all!) when interviewed?

Easter Bonnets

I love the Easter
Congregation:
New bonnets, beauty
And salvation

Make you think just why
Dress up the body,
Which for forty days of Lent
Was shoddy.

But look! His rising up
Is pledge to be
Of body glorious.
I think I see:

Agile body, go where e're
You will.
Impassible, never feel
An ill.

Brightful, beauteous body, star out-
Shining star;
And subtle body, soul commanding,
Not as now we are.

With all this promised us
(His word upon it!),
Dress up your body, Christian soul,
In Easter bonnet!

Boats

Some day I'd like to have a little boat
All to myself.
Her cabin bare, a simple galley
And a shelf
To hold a few good books.
The smell
Of tidal water, and the slap
And swell
A neighbor passing by caused up.
To pass
An island by and stop or no.
A sea bass
For my supper, rudely cooked.
The red
Of sunset sets alarm—but I
Abed.
There's something faintly Christian
In these gloats:
Or what would heaven be for Peter, Andrew, James and
    John
Without boats?

Sweet Defeat

An hour ago
I thought I saw
The world in focus:
Awful awe!

The ringing phone,
Another's woes
Spoiled the focus...
So it goes.

Xavier Dreams

Billows from the Orient, kissed by moonlight,
Silhouetted galleon riding down the bay,
    Speak to him of journeys
    Distant, toilsome,
Back to whitened fields in rich Cathay!

Breezes from the Orient, softly playing,
Rustling in the palm trees, whispering low,
    Breathe of dim pagodas,
    Burning incense,
Breathe of grinning idols row on row.

Storm clouds from the Orient, black and boding,
Coming round the Cape in huge black rolls,
    Rumble tales of dragons,
    Gongs and chanting,
Rumble tales of sin and yellow men's souls!

John XXIII

Big-eared and violent-nosed,
With sad, sad, searching eyes
And gentle woman's mouth.
The heart within him bursting all the bounds
His dumpy little body can endure.
Thick ankles and tired feet bestride
Two worlds, and even enemies bow down in love.
Peter I was clumsy, tactless, smelled of fish.
But Peter had a heart.
So John XXIII.

Who's a Saint?

The saint's the guy that walks the street with you,
Drinks, picks up the tab,
Goes home and loves his wife,
And children,
And all the world.

Don't tell me saints are only those that sit in cloisters.
Saints love God.
And because they do
They love the rest of us,
It's true!

Aetas Senescit

An old man goes to seed?
Oh, no!

He's spent his need:
it's so.

Now, like a weed
To blow?

Or like a reed
To glow?

Quatrain with a Cancerous Third Line

Around, around
Your world does go,
Of protons, neutrons, atoms, travelling
    in field subservient, and always
    obedient, crumblingly, fumblingly
    organized, among which helter skelter
    I alone
Can answer no!

Selfhood

Oh, men will reach the stars
And someday someone round the sun will ride;
Despite their calculated nears and fars
The stars I reach for are inside.

I Like This World

Some think the universe a joke
Despite the orchid, fern and oak;
I think the world is wondrous still
Because it's full of Jack and Jill.

So little in my inward, kinward, sinward world
Stand they:
When most I needed them,
They turned away.

"Saints"

Pietitis makes me wroth
(Those sad, ecstatic plaints)
Dear Lord, I cherish holy men,
But spare me, Lord, from "Saints"!

My Morning Meditation? Lord,
Forgive my thoughts for erring so:
Would Joseph, carpenter, have joined
The A.F.L. or C.I.O.?

To Coeds Everywhere

How sweet you look, high-heeled, and gussied up
On Sunday.
You ought to see yourselves, still sweet, unheeled, at eight
On Monday.

Well?

How silly "names"
Celebrities and such,
Which, cashed with other chips,
Don't matter much.

I Am

I am (I hear it ring!)
Such a nothing!

Yawn

I had not yawned for months
And now I yawn.
Goodness, gracious,
It's almost dawn.

OF NATURE

September 15

The leaves still green
And nothing really changed
By more than you can tell the age
Of someone over twenty-nine
But surely under thirty.
Just hinted on the air a wisp of musk,
As when you bow before the lady just approached.
A breath of wind.
Just over twenty-nine
And surely under thirty.

Spring

Spring enters like a girl into a room:
Her crocus-tentative, shy opening of the door,
Her daffodillic suddenness in bloom,
Her hyacinthine walk across the floor,
Her first word, as the new birds sing at dawn,
Her warmth at meeting you, like elm buds sprung,
Her easeful beautifulness, like greening lawn,
Her growing old so soon, and she so young.

Non Bona Fides

Urgently at work the frost
Fulfills his demolition job, a cost-
Plus contract: spoil all around
Whatever can be found above the ground.

No cost to him, the plus is borne by us.
Frost executes his contract without fuss.
His bill presented, we reluctant pay,
Not knowing how he bilked us until May.

The Buttercup

Angered hands reach down
To pluck it up.
Angered hands should not pluck up
A buttercup.

Milan (Washington) in Late September

The mountains thunder
Me under.
Louring, gold-green
And green-gold, and tamracked, and yellow-gold,
And green firred, and yellow, yellow, yellow, old,
And never really ever seen:
Yellow, yellow, yellow and dull red
When summer's sped.
I smell
The wet draw
Where cedars dwell
Ah!
I kiss
Earth's bliss.

To My Window

The equinoctial wind blows hard;
My window's open on the yard,
And leaning out I feel the kiss
Of reaching April's lips and bliss.

All winter, tight against the storm,
My window schemed and kept me warm.
Ungrateful I, as you I raise,
For what you have kept out I praise.

The Drop

I

Swelling
From the earth like a drop of woman's milk,
Welling
Up in sweetness, shadowed under silk
Of light,
Swooped at by a dragonfly, the drop
Takes flight
Over the lip and down the flute to stop,
First pooled.
Phantom, quick, dart of darkness,
A trout
Smoothes itself against the drop (the starkness
Of doubt
Made clear: a drop of water and the living can unite)
Until
A puzzled, struggling fly, a conquered mite
Is still
In the swelling power of water. So
A creek.
The surge of its first cascade, to grow
Like squeak
Of boy who makes his man's first syllable:
Escape
The gulp into a gulf unfillable
Of shape
Of casual, thirsty cow; then round a ridge
By farm
And under sagged, log-stringered bridge.
Alarm!

Identity is lost, the river sucks into
Its sweep
The drop: sad anonymity,
As weep
All multituded men. But, see
The move
Of all about is somehow slowed,
To prove
That multituded might can be allowed
Or not
At all. The first strong dam!

II

Then shot
With sudden, awful, sickening fling
Down, down
(Memory of the fetal drop from spring!)
To drown
And out and tear and roar and smash—
Somehow,
By shouldering with them, *the lightning flash!*
But now
Loitering, but shouldering still,
Weak drop
Supports the moving tons from mill
And crop.
Swept toward the city, where from other springs
Comes more
Of water seeking, blind, on broken wings
The shore.
The city laves and bathes itself and leaves
Its stinks,
Its awful offalness of petty peeves:
It drinks
Of its own awfulness. But on,
Now calm,
Its old age dirtied, as men bear dirt in age:
The balm

Of tide, the last anointing, rage
Of bar
Of judgment just ahead: fog,
No star.
Fresh naïveté is bitter salted—log
It. But
Lost freshness finds a newness in the salt.
God, what
To be at last in deeps, at peace, and without fault!

Evolution

Little fish in water, go,
Aged a million years or so.

Little man upon the bank,
Who uprose while others sank.

Beauty, startling, in the brook,
Living rainbow as I look.

Hardly beauty standing here
Ecstasized by you! It's queer

And awfully shaking, but it's true
That I'm the one that writes of you!

From Azzurbano

I'll write to you from Azzurbano
How the goats and kidlets do,
Whether grass on alto plano
Lasts the season; whether, too,

Church bells ring, as when we walking
Saw the earth so much in tune:
Church bells ringing, children playing, talking,
Talking just in June.

I love the newer muse:
Its formless fire
Its gustful writhings
Like a cable twisted taut between
Two engines, slacked and taut again.

I do not laugh
I wonder at its life. Is it
Life that springs from newer birth,
Like that life of water and the Ghost
Which ruptures ties of lazy sin
Resurgent and new?

Or life that lingers in the anarchic cells
After the soul departs,
Disparate, disintegrate,
Lacking end and meaning?

I love the newer muse.
Its formless fire and writings
Not for itself—itself it's ugly
But for that it presages
Chrysalis—like the damp and quivering velvet
Of the parent moth.

The Road

I found a road this summer day
Which no one else
Had walked down for some time.
A spray
Of elderberry gathered dust.
And by the road
Were rusting strands of barbed wire.
Away
Across the meadow calf and cow
Were eating of the grass they did not grow.
As I walked down the road I did not build
Today.

The Mountain

How upward, soaring, dwarfing
Stands yon hill,
And after I am gone
It will rise still.
But all it is and has been, can be, will
Be, is far less than I.
I talk of it which cannot talk of me,
Is why.

To Fall

How graciously has summer flown
The ballroom, where her scent is blown
Upon the draft the closing door
Of her departure stirs once more.

And we who waltzed with her are left
With empty arms and rue the theft
Which leaves us standing, wondering
If she and we shall dance next spring.

Change

How anguished dawns arise
And burst the skies
And sunsets furious to leave
Beg reprieve
Until tomorrow.

Come and go
Is sorrow.

Height Psychology

Height psychology
Is fine,
It structures to
The divine.
It proves the world can do
Without
The
Umlaut.

Beauty

Beauty's by the road,
Or on a bush,
Or on two feet.
Beauty is a goad.
So hush,
Until we meet.

In Trium

A pansy just at dawn,
A spindle-legged fawn,
A field of wheat in June,
A flock of robins new in tune,
A pregnant woman proud
(A judgment not allowed!),
A bowed-head penitent,
A salmon spent:
All these, my divine and dainty Trinity,
Are like Thee,
Three.

"April is the cruelest month."
I wonder really why.
Because it bridges angry March and lovely May
And quickly passes by?

It Is a Question

Even this earth is a wearyful wanderer,
Using up space. To what profitable end?
In all this majestical: weary, I, wanderer,
Ask why and how you picked me as your friend.

Amoeba

Elemental, subdivided,
Half in two,
When you've done, just who decided
Which is you?

Moon on Ice

Dead white moon,
Which sets on fire a lake of ice,
I hope to see, Aroon,
Such beauty twice.

Delight of Memory

I heard
A bird
Afterward.

In Resurrectionem Mortuorum

"Matter matters," said my friend,
As hundreds to him listened.
And, while he spoke of matter's end,
Man, work, trees, flowers glistened.

About in me the atoms played,
Neutrons without exemption,
Which will, if they in me have stayed,
Partake of the Redemption.

July 19

Who builds the summer:
Leaves, sheaves, beeves?
Who takes it back,
And also leaves?

Snowflake

A flake of dye from the burdened sky
    I tinge the earth below
And downy white steal through the night—
    Like dreams I come and go.
The ruined shroud of a shimmering cloud
    I muffle the world in sleep,
The trees caress with drowsiness
    As they ghostlike vigils keep.
A wraithy pearl, I skim and swirl
    On the wings of the lullaby wind
And drifting down the mountains crown
    With the garland I've left behind.
And after my life of frozen strife
    With a mocking laugh I flee,
And crystal shape make my escape
    In the depths of the crystal sea!

OF GOD

To The Holy Ghost and Hope

The trace of You in all this world
Is just a smidgeon:
Our only glimpse of You
Is wind and pigeon.

And so with faith and hope and charity—
Hope hides so shy;
Believing, loving we use hope
Until we die.

And so you both, forgotten ones of three,
Dear You and hope,
Without You and Your wondrous gift
We grope.

The Blind Man of Jericho

Ah, blind, my friend,
You little man of Joshua's town
Beside the stream. The bend
The road makes and the last steps down
To the beach your whole sure world.
Beyond that, nothing. Hush, a man comes by, he…
Ah, do you see?
Do you *see!*

To God

There's nothing in Your world I want: not money,
To be loved, be duke or earl, or even honorable.
Everything, if loved beside You, taints.
I want to be
The meanest, least, most ragged of Your saints.

Fiat

The less I say
The more I grow:
God's example
Makes it so.

One word he said
And all began,
Uncomfortably
Including man.

Had he said less
I would not be:
Say just enough,
But carefully.

Playthings

I found a child who had three things:
A Noah's Ark, A Cross, and something small that sings.

His Noah's Ark is drowned and long since gone.
His Cross is on some others' shoulders proudly on.

The singing thing he then possessed (go Caiphus, and whip
and tree)
The singing thing he had, and has, and will have: me!

On Daily Communion

Yes, there are those that once a year
Receive and so fulfil the law;
And there those in higher gear
Who every Sunday go, and without flaw.

And other some go every day, odd,
Turning Christ to self,
Embezzlers of God's grace and God
And other pelf.

The Judgment

When I die, God the Father's going to say;
"Sit down, for God's sake (That's We)
Relax
And get the load off of your feet.
My Son will get around to you
In a minute."

About Being Christ

We trim our toes,
Did you?

We blow our nose,
Did you?

How many fervent Christians
Over-niced
Realize it took some doing
To be Christ!

After a Philomathea Meeting

Suppose that de Chardin is right:
The universe goes on in ever better case.
So what's to do when humans see the light
Supernal, looking at the Threesome face to face?

Will God still call for volunteers to man
The various concerns this universe entails,
To join with St. Therése in doing good, and span
The coming centuries in seeing nothing fails?

Will some saints moonlight? Taking time from rest?
So electronics fall to Hubert's watchful care?
And secondary boosters Anselm's charge? Who's best
For transportation round the sun? Who'll share

In supervising cosmic A & P? Will de Lillis
Handle hospitals in space? And will I feel my oats
By being put in charge of things for Phyllis,
Needles, pins, and lace, and J. P. Coates?

Annunciation Morn

'Twas dawn!
Night's ghost had fled,
And in the purple-draperied West
Whence truant stars
Were sped
Adown the skyey pathways of the Morn,
The morning-moon
In filmy bridals dressed
Slow, slow sank
Unto her bed,
While forth in geysers bright
A thousand dawn-fonts spumed
Their saffron light
To bathe in liquid glory
Day
New-born!

Across the dewy lawn
Of lovely Galilee,
From out the caves of dawn
An angel
Sped as free
As cloud-wisps flung before the mad March wind
Anon
On spirit feet
Anon
More wildly fleet
Than moonbeams on a mountain rill
He sped,
Nor stayed him till
Without an open window
By a flowering tamerind
He stopped
To loose his star-soiled sandals e'er
He cross a maiden's sill!

Lo,
Soft
An amber glow the chamber fills,
The suitor pleads;
Nor is denied;
The maiden's voice
Is heard:
"Be it done as to thy word"—
God becomes enfleshed—
Man deified!

O Mother and Inviolate,
Virgin and she
Who didst conceive and usher forth
The Christ,
Thou limpid, fruitful font of Sanctity
Whence sprang the Crimson Flood,
Our Eucharist:
Thou tryst
Of age-old hopes and irised covenant.
Thou crystal mirror of the Ageless Face,
The Which reflecting,
Thou didst so enchant
Thy formless, light-winged visitant
That from his angel-heart there burst the cry:
"Hail, full of grace"...

Ah,
Hear anew that Ave's simple laud
Which first a poet-angel sang;
Beloved of God, let that sweet prayer
Breathe forth my love—
For thou, O Mary, God-beloved,
Thou hast trove
Far
Far beyond my humble plighting:
For thou art
Deipotent with Love divine,
And hast God's Heart,
Yet...
Wouldst thou mine?

To God

Strange, but right
My odd, odd view
Of
You.

I hold
Orthodoxly
You are
True.

I know your trueness,
I can taste it, I,
So that
I cry.

Love of God

If you're in love with God
It shows;
Something inward
Glows.

Inwardly there is
A vision;
Stop
Derision.

The Ballad of the Lake

"I go a fishing," Peter saith,
    "We also come with thee."
And forth they went, as oft before,
    On sparkling Galilee.

And all that night they plied their nets
    Beneath the moon's soft ray,
But angels swam before their skiff
    And shooed the fish away.

And when the sun peeped o'er the hills
    From out the Arab sea,
Behold, a Man stood on the shore
    Close by a cypress tree.

"Children, have ye aught of meat?"
    "Alas!" the seven sighed...
The Stranger smiled and called again;
    "Cast on the other side!"

They cast and, lo, their nets were filled
    An hundred fifty-three!
But John who caught the Stranger's smile
    First knew that it was He.

Now, I love to stand upon the shore
    At dawn that fresh spring day,
And ponder (smiling to myself)
    The joke the Lord did play!

Only Mind Can Praise

How grand
I stand
Derivatively
Imitatively
You.
And all things yours
Creatively,
Earth's furnitures,
Go through
Me back to You, the Word, the Thought,
Or ought
To.
Well,
Only men face hell
Among things which or who
Calling
Falling
Die.
So odd,
Dear God,
That little I
Of all your cure
Am for them your
Why!

To the Trinity

How dangerously
You, wise, remake yourselves through men;
You, Father, Son and Holy Ghost
Through such as me. Amen.

Priest at Communion

Handle Beauty
Without breaking?
Human hand
Is shaking.

Shaking hand
In human mouths
Peddles Beauty,
As by vows.

When I Am Bent

God's will, which cannot bend
Or bent be,
Is loved by me.
The end
Of all His great conniving is that He
And I agree.

Vision

I saw a rose:
It goes.

I saw a rainbow bent:
It's spent.

I saw a woman smile
Awhile.

I saw enticingly
Just Thee.

Incarnatum

Darkness
Had to do
With
Something new.

Too long
Had anger curled
Against
The world.

This new,
Hereto unsaid,
Unspeaking,
Hath visited.

To God, My Love

Always nothing,
Cosmic cypher,
Watching while from out you flow
All these wondrously wrought beings.
I am *ens ab alio*.

Take me, little cypher,
Make me darkly to your own intent.
Make me love you as you love me.
Bend me, break me,
Leave me bent.

Round Despair

Devil damn you, dismal, deviating
Bill;
On the other hand, there's God who loves you
Still.

To God

Glorious God
In afterview
How very much
I'm not like you.

To Christ

Hanging on your cross
You are absurd:
Goodness,
My Word!

I think I am a
Very odd
Image
of God

To God Again

So very much I want to flee
All men
To be
With all You Three.
Amen.

Straw Words

"Twas afternoon. The dim old halls
of the convent echoed the silent hour;
in the cloister-walk a footstep falls—
a friar and his beads. The shuttered tower
of the convent church is hushed in prayer
for white-cowled doves tell vespers there.

Alone and unmoved in his tiny cell
a huge man sits, and the tip of his quill
makes a sign on his lips: nor the vesper bell
he hears, for the depths of his thought are still
And the gaze of his eyes grows far away:
the depths of seas in their misty grey!

Beyond, far beyond his thoughts are spanned,
and his eyes are fixed to the onyx Throne
where sits the Son at Father's hand;
and behold! he is there a man alone
with the thoughts of Deity—close to Him,
more close than the jealous seraphim!

Dumb as an ox he ponders there
what none has seen, nor any heard:
content as an ox to stand and stare
at the Maker, the Ghost and the Word!
(...But the supper bell has long since rung,
and the cloister lamps have long been hung.)

And still the huge man sits alone,
dumb as an ox; in ecstasy
he hears from the Throne:
"Thomas thou has writ well of Me!"
(...But a friar comes in and shakes his chair
and wonders he sits so silent there.)

The books he's writ, his treatises,
he smiles—pages of oaten straw;
foolish the words and useless these
the senseless notes of a raucous daw.
(...The prior, Brother Thomas, would speak with thee,
the Summa is done and he fain would see!

Come, Brother Thomas 'tis past the hour!
and nothing to writ? thy quill still dry?
Hear, Brother Thomas, the bell in the tower
rings out; stars grow dim in the morning sky!)
And Thomas looks up; and nods, and then
he crumples his paper, and breaks his pen.

OF DEATH

Necrography

For thirty minutes after death God gave
(By way of penance for my sins and way to save
My soul from loss of what I'd longed to see)
An awful task: "Write down," he said, "the things you've
    done for me."
So there I was, hunched over at my desk,
My elbow pressing keys: xzmyrtyu. Statuesque
Until they found me. But a final theme to write!
What should, could, would, can, may, or will or might?
A blind but first time seeing eye looked round about
The utter clutter of my life, my desk: the stout
And broken-bounden book of sixteenth-century poetry
I took (marked "Reference") from the library,
Bottles of pills and dried-up milk of bismuth, and a pen
I meant to get a refill for, next year's catalog unchecked,
    again
As yet again the manuscript I'd vowed to see in print,
That book review, half-written, somehow never jelled, a hint
I'd written to the Rector (never sent), and photographs I'd
    meant to send
To all my sisters (my sad, ingrate persona with them mend),
Some Dentyne gum unchewed, a half-filled pack of ciga-
    rettes.
The useless travel-pack my razor came in, and regrets

For papers uncorrected, and March and April dates down in
    my book,
The brochure, *Stately British Homes*, at which I'd meant to
    look,
An article on *Hamlet*, once-rejected, meant to be put right,
The cuff-links, Christmas present, not yet written thanks,
And little poems, half-written, half-ideas, blanks...
So God said: "All you did were always things undone.
Well, come along with Us, and have some fun."

Death

I dread the black eternity,
Although I know the Father,
Son, and
Holy Ghost await me there.
How hard to leave this world,
So colored and so full of sound,
And full of smell!
Colored, soundful, smellful world—
Nothing like the world which waits with
Them.

"Who Shall I Say is Calling?"

He rapped upon the Palace gate,
    A tattered vagabond was he:

And to the puzzled warden said,
    "I knew your Lord—we died at three!"

About Death

When you come
I shall be alone
Withering
Unknown.

Around maybe
Are all I've loved before;
With them thee
I adore.

To a Dear Friend Dead

Farewell, dear goodbyed friend;
Our earth is by you less,
And heaven is, I guess,
A place more lovely. End
Of all of us who weep,
And fearful dread the sleep.
But sleep's to wake, my friend.

Cancer

A length of waiting, endlessly
The hours are suicides; and she
Can only wait, the same as we.

Her breath is harder; sleep is hard,
Her body dry, a fragile shard
Of human kind. Respect the card:

"No Visitors. Do Not Disturb."
For her no rest from mine or herb.
She gasps. God put to pain a curb.

You wisemen, you who tell us how
To live from forty on, say now
How human nature knows to bow.

Speak up! The wise return your gaze;
The wiser ones an eyebrow raise;
The wisest one is one who prays
   God give her rest.

Just As If

When I was on earth
I liked it there;
I much prefer it
Here.

Death

Out of the darkness
Out of the gloom
Sudden in starkness
(Wide is the room)
Despite the hierarchness
Bride and bridegroom!

This must be almost the last poem Father Costello wrote. He gave it to me with two others during the Easter vacation of 1963. On the morning vacation ended he was found unconscious, in a coma from which he never fully recovered until he died two weeks later on May 5th, 1963.

Charles Keenan, S.J.